EARTHWISE

My Town

Pam Robson

Stargazer Books

CONTENTS

© Aladdin Books Ltd 2005

First published in the
United States in 2005 by:
Stargazer Books
c/o The Creative Company
123 South Broad Street
P.O. Box 227
Mankato, Minnesota 56002

All rights reserved

Printed in U.A.E.

Editor
Jim Pipe

Educational Consultant
Jackie Holderness

Design
Flick, Book Design and
Graphics

Picture Research
Brian Hunter Smart

Library of Congress
Cataloging-in-Publication Data

Robson, Pam.
  My town / by Pam Robson.
    p. cm.-- (Earthwise)
  Includes index.
  ISBN 1-932799-49-4 (alk paper)
    1. Cities and towns--Juvenile literature.
    2. Municipal services--Juvenile
  literature. 3. Community life--Juvenile
  literature. I. Title. II. Series.

HT152.R63 2004
307.76--dc22   2004042880

INTRODUCTION

A long time ago, people learned to live together in places that were safe from enemies and where there was food and water. People now live in groups close to where they work. We may live in a small town or a big city, but we make life easier by living and working with other people.

HOW TO USE THIS BOOK

Watch for the symbol of the magnifying glass for tips on what to look for in your town or city.

The paintbrush boxes contain activities that relate to your locality, the place where you live.

WHERE YOU LIVE

Whether you live in a small town or a big city, most people around you organize their lives in a similar way. A settled group of people is called a community. Everyone in a community needs a home, somewhere to work, a place to shop, and a place to have fun. They share services such as buses, schools, and hospitals.

Places where people have settled are called settlements. We call small settlements (top) villages and large settlements towns (right) or cities.

People have settled in many different places. Coastal settlements are built by the sea. Towns and villages are even found on mountaintops.

My Home

Many artists have painted pictures of their home. What do you like best about the place where you live? Is it the shape or color of the building? Paint a picture of your home. You may have a favorite room or a favorite view out of a window.

Bedroom at Arles by Vincent van Gogh

All settlements need utilities, such as electricity and water, and services, such as post offices and mass transit.

A city has many kinds of transit, such as trains, buses, and taxis. But in a village (above), a bus may go to the nearest town only once a day.

DIFFERENT • AREAS

Your town may have separate areas for living, working, shopping, or having fun. These often include apartment blocks, industrial parks, shopping malls, and sports centers. Some towns have pedestrian precincts just for people on foot. Is there an area like this near you?

HOUSES AND HOMES

Homes provide shelter. Modern houses also have access to utilities like water and electricity so that people can cook, eat, and keep clean (left). But if your home is built in a remote place, it may not have access to all these utilities. The kind of house in which people live also depends upon where they live and what they can afford.

H OUSE • TYPES

People live in homes of different sizes and styles. Look in your local area for row houses (above), apartments, and ranch houses (houses with no stairs).

Cottages, Houses, and Apartments
In the countryside, cottages are often far apart. In towns, people may live closer together in joined houses called rows. Tall apartment blocks are found in crowded cities around the world (above).

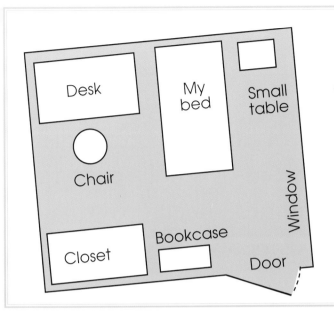

My Room

Most homes have different rooms or areas for eating, sleeping, washing, and relaxing. Draw a plan of your bedroom. If you know how to draw a plan to scale, measure the length and width of the room. Mark the position of the door, windows, and furniture.

Homes on Water

People build homes to suit where they live. This coastal village in the Philippines (above) is built on stilts, to protect it from floods. In Hong Kong, some families, called "boat people," live on boats in the harbor.

On the Move

Some people, called "nomads," choose not to settle. They travel from place to place and take their homes with them. Refugees are people forced to move due to wars or famine. They often have to live in crowded camps.

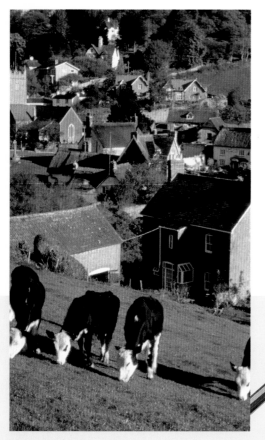

VILLAGES

Villages around the world look different because of differences in climate, landscape, and local building materials.

Many villages begin as small farming or fishing communities. They grow slowly over time as people settle in them.

AROUND • THE • WORLD

Using books and the internet, compare three villages from around the world. Find out what houses look like, what jobs people do, and what services there are.

Village in England

The weather can be cold in England. Houses protect against wind and rain. Villagers have access to electricity and water. But there are not always local stores and post offices. Many villagers now work in nearby towns.

Village in Southern Italy

Houses here protect against the hot summer sun. Villagers can still find work on local farms where crops such as olives and lemons are grown.

Basic Services

Villages in developing parts of the world have few services. The United Nations and other organizations are working to provide all children with clean water, schools, and basic healthcare. Use the internet to find out about Universal Children's Day.

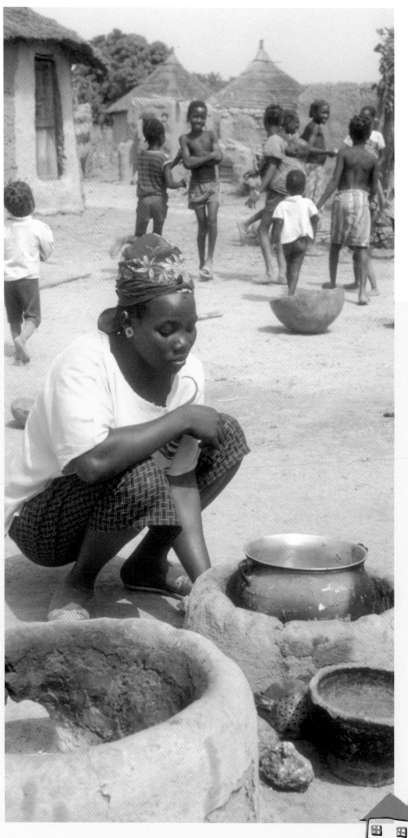

Village in Mali, West Africa

The climate in Mali is warm, but in the summer there are heavy rains. Most villages are farming or fishing communities. The houses are built from mud and villages have few services or decent roads. In Ouellessebougou village (right), the electricity is switched on for just a few hours each day. The village school was built with money raised by children from another country.

TOWNS

Towns are larger than villages and smaller than cities. In addition to a place to live, most towns provide jobs, stores, hospitals, schools, and fun things for people to do on the weekend. A town may also provide these services for neighboring villages. Many villages depend upon towns for things that they need.

T OWN • WILDLIFE

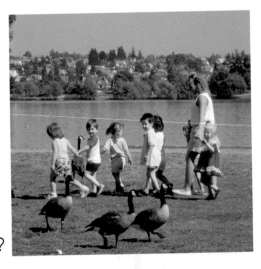

Wild animals, such as birds and squirrels, have adapted to town (urban) life. Town planners also help wildlife by leaving areas of land between large towns. This is called "greenbelt" land. Look out for wildlife in your area and record your observations. Can you name the birds that you see?

Old and New

Towns usually have a function. This means that they are built for a reason. A long time ago, castle settlements were built in places that were safe from enemies.

Market Towns

Many towns grew from country villages where there was a market. Even in large towns, farmers may still bring their animals and crops to sell in a weekly market.

Trading Towns

Many old towns grew up along main trading routes. Some developed around railroads, others around harbors, or along rivers.

Industrial Centers

Many new towns grow up around factories where goods are made, or where there are natural resources, such as oil or coal.

CITIES

Many of the world's largest cities have a lot in common. They have skyscrapers and subways (underground railroads). Big companies sell their goods all over the world, so similar names appear on the stores in many cities. Some businesses are open all day and night. In a big city, it is never completely dark at night. Neon city lights blot out the light from the stars.

C ROWDS

A city grows because people move there to find jobs or because they want to live in a place with lots of services. If you visit a big city, see if downtown is crowded (right). As a city grows, people move to new homes on the outskirts, called "suburbs." A growing city often "swallows up" smaller towns nearby.

Landmarks

All cities have important public buildings, such as government offices, places of worship, and libraries. If you visit a big city, you can buy postcards of your favorite places. Send one to a friend describing what you have seen.

On the outskirts of some large cities, poorer families have built homes for themselves next to the homes of the rich. In Sao Paolo (Brazil) and Nairobi (Kenya), the poor live in homes like this. These areas are called "shantytowns." Homes are built using junk or discarded materials.

FARMS

Cities and towns rely on farmers to provide them with food. Farmers work on the land, growing crops, and raising animals for food. Animals, such as sheep, also provide fibers such as wool (right). This is spun and woven into material for clothing.

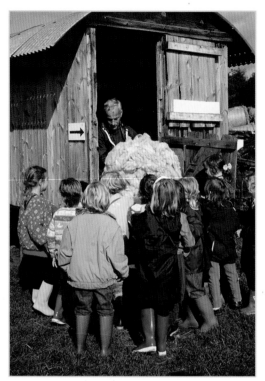

Wool comes from sheep.

In the past, many farmers in North America and Europe lived and worked on their own farms. Today, these farms are often owned by large cooperatives that pay people to work on their land.

Where From?

Look at food labels on the fruit and vegetables in your local supermarket. Many have come from far away. Make a list of the countries where these fruits and vegetables were grown. Use an atlas to locate these places.

PLANTATIONS

A plantation is a farm that employs many workers to grow one crop, such as tea, coffee, or bananas (below). The workers often work very hard for very little money. Look on a jar of coffee or a box of tea. You will see that they are grown in tropical (warm) climates, in countries such as India and Colombia.

Some families in developing countries live on very small farms where they only grow enough food to feed themselves and their animals. They do not grow enough food to sell. This is called subsistence farming.

GOING TO WORK

Workers in many towns and cities find jobs in local factories. A factory is a place of work where raw materials are made into the goods you buy in stores. For example, potatoes are made into chips in a chip factory. Workers use machines to make a large number of similar goods very quickly.

Changing Jobs

Until recently, people who went out to work expected to do the same job for life. Now, workers often change jobs. Talk to your grandparents or other older people you know about the jobs that they have had. What changes have they seen happening?

In developing countries, workers (who may be children) work long hours for very little money. They make clothes and household items that are sold for high prices in other countries.

F ACTORIES

Look at an up-to-date map of where you live to find out whether there are any factories in your area. Can you find out what is made there?

Larger factories are often built in industrial parks on the outskirts of towns. Smoke from factories once caused air pollution. Today, most factories must use clean electric power.

If a factory closes down, many people will become unemployed (left without work). In some parts of the world, there are fewer and fewer jobs in older industries such as shipbuilding, steel making, and coal mining. Workers must learn new skills to work in service jobs, or move to other towns to find work.

TOWN SERVICES

If your mom or dad works in an office (below), they probably work in a service job. Services provide settlements with basic utilities such as clean water, heating, and lighting.

However, many other services are needed in a modern town, from banks, schools, and hospitals to cinemas, playgrounds, and libraries.

There are still communities in the world that have no running water or electricity. Water must be collected from standpipes or wells (above) several times every day.

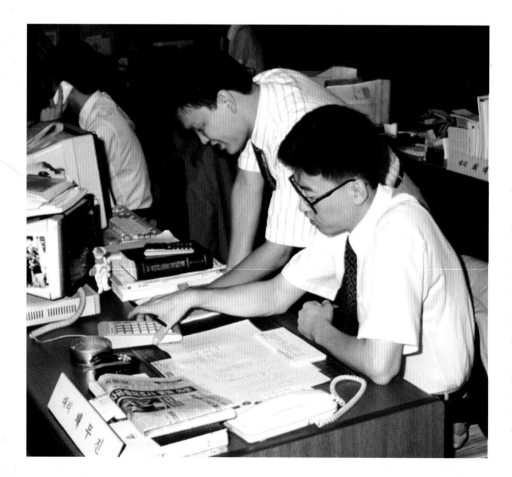

We all take basic services, such as clean water and electricity, for granted. Imagine your home with no electric power. There would be no television, no microwave, and no light. Power failures can plunge whole cities into darkness.

Water/sewage

Power/lighting

Hospitals

Communications

Investigating a manhole

Services Map

With a friend, search for clues about services in your locality. You could look for water and electricity supplies (manholes and overhead cables). You could also watch for signs of communications, such as telephone wires, mailboxes, cellphone masts, and TV aerials.

Then look for banks and stores, and leisure services such as parks, playgrounds, movie theaters, and sports centers. Make up symbols for these places or objects. Then mark them on a photocopy of a local map.

Post office

Stores

Parks/playgrounds

Museums/galleries

ALL CHANGE!

Is someone always digging up the roads near you (right)? All towns change as they grow. New homes replace old ones. Superstores replace small stores. Local councils must repair or widen roads as more and more cars and trucks use them.

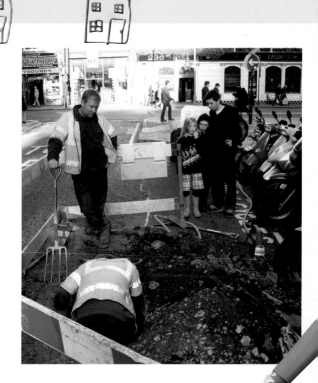

The names of cities and towns can even change. This is especially true in India. The city of Bombay is now Mumbai. The city of Calcutta is now called Kolkata. Madras has been renamed Chennai. Can you locate these cities on the globe?

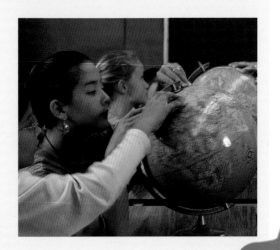

Let Them Know

Write a letter to your local council suggesting improvements you would like to see in your locality. Are the roads dangerous because there is too much traffic? You might suggest speed restrictions or pedestrian areas. Perhaps the children in your area need a new playground.

T OWN • COUNCILS

The town council is responsible for the day-to-day care of your locality. Look out for council employees at work. You may see them collecting trash (above), sweeping the streets, looking after parks (right), mending street lights, and repairing roads. The council also pays specialist firms to do these jobs for them.

GETTING AROUND

Every community needs a good transit system. You need to travel to school and your family needs to get to work. Goods have to be transported to stores and factories. Some people commute (travel daily) to work over long distances on trains and in cars. Airports provide links to other countries, allowing people to travel quickly all over the world. The world seems to have become smaller.

Airports and railroad stations are busy terminals for journeys to and from places near and far. Highways carry streams of cars and trucks between large towns and cities.

This traffic flows around the outside of small settlements along roads called beltways. This reduces traffic in villages and towns, making them quieter and less polluted.

Traffic Survey

Cars and trucks pollute the air. Carry out a traffic survey with a friend, in a street close to home or school. Record the number of vehicles that pass you in an hour. How many create dirty fumes? Which ones are noisy?

A ROUND • TOWN

High speed subways carry passengers beneath cities. Cars, buses, and taxis move along networks of streets.

If you are in a city or busy town, look around you. Observe the different types of transportation in use. Depending on where you are, people may travel on bicycles, in rickshaws, or high in the air along monorails. Large towns may also have a train or tram service.

Monorail

Rickshaw

COMPARING TOWNS

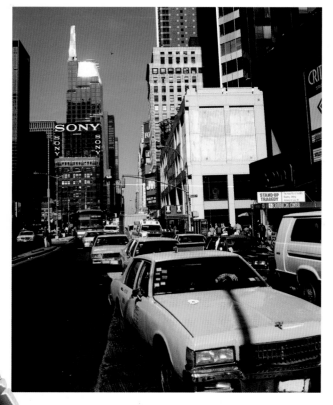

Most people travel at some point in their lives, even if they only visit the nearest big town or city once or twice a year. They also travel to take vacations, or to visit family and friends. As we move around, we may visit towns that are different from our home, such as ports or vacation resorts.

Change of Scene

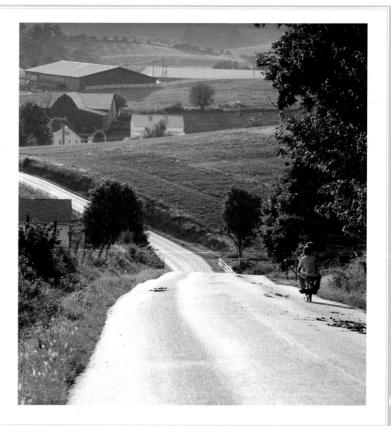

Imagine what it is like for someone who usually lives in the country to travel to a big city (above). Or, if you live in a busy city, write a story about what it might be like for someone who usually lives in the country (right). What do you think is different about the buildings, the numbers of people, the noises and smells, and the wildlife they might see?

VACATION • HELP

Next time you go on vacation, keep a record of all the people who help you with your travel plans. Travel agents, hotel staff, waiters, store assistants, airport staff, and taxi drivers are all people who provide services.

More and more people now travel around the world for their vacations. There are many different resorts to be visited. Vacation destinations may be chosen because of their scenery, their climate, or their sights and attractions.

There may also be facilities for sports, such as skiing on snow-covered mountains, or surfing on coastal waters.

When a village becomes popular with tourists, it can grow very quickly. There are **seaside resorts** (left) all over the world. Many began as small fishing villages.

Many snow-covered mountain villages become popular ski resorts during the winter months.

Firefighter

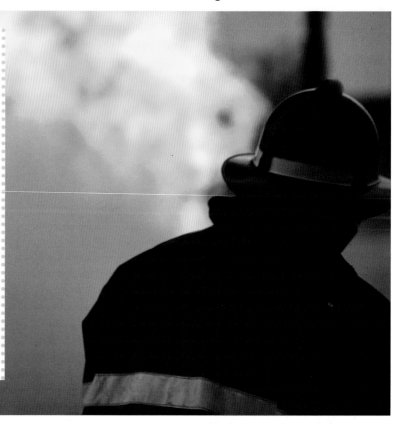

EMERGENCY

Modern towns and cities have emergency services that respond in a disaster. People call the fire service when a fire or explosion occurs. You, too, should know what to do in an emergency. Ask a parent or teacher to show you what to do and where to go.

Ambulance crew

A SAFE PLACE TO LIVE

Everyone needs to feel safe. Natural disasters like hurricanes, earthquakes, and floods can destroy homes and cause deaths.

However, flood barriers can hold back high tides on large rivers. Along many coasts, sea walls protect us from stormy seas. If a disaster happens, people help each other. Police cars, fire engines, and ambulances rush to the scene of an emergency. They rescue people in danger.

Earthquakes

In regions prone to earthquakes, buildings are often designed to withstand the force of an earthquake. However, strong earthquakes can destroy buildings, bridges, and roads, leaving many people homeless.

Floods

People have always chosen to live near water. But homes built on the flood plains of rivers like the Mississippi or the Yangtse (in China), need flood defenses. High tides and heavy rainfall can raise the water level and flood houses.

Volcanoes

Settlements standing beneath active volcanoes have been buried beneath rivers of lava. In 1902, Mount Pelee, on the Caribbean island of Martinique, erupted. In the valley below, 30,000 people died in the town of St. Pierre.

OUR ENVIRONMENT

People need a healthy environment to live in. The environment is everything around us, including the air, water, plants, and the buildings we live in. No one likes noisy streets or breathing in dirty car fumes all day, so parks are as important to a town as buildings. But all towns create trash and pollution that can damage our environment.

Wildlife Parks

People need to learn how to live with nature. One answer is to provide homes for local wildlife in parks and gardens. Many countries also make important habitats (animal homes) into wildlife parks. One of the most famous is Yellowstone National Park (right). Many parks have special rules to protect the animals and plants that live there. No settlements can be built in a wildlife park.

GARBAGE • DUMPS

People produce mountains of garbage. A lot of this is packaging from goods made in factories. Many councils bury trash underground, in sites called "landfills." Find out what happens to the trash in your area.

Be a good citizen and encourage your family to sort its trash before throwing it away. Use the recycling containers in your locality. Separate glass, paper, aluminum, and plastic. Many materials can be recycled. See how much your family can recycle in a month.

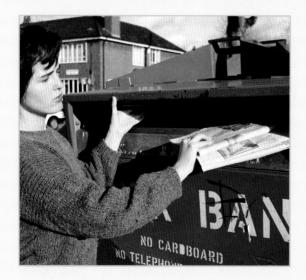

USEFUL WORDS

citizen—a member of a community who has certain rights in return for being a responsible member of the community.

communications—the things that help us talk or pass information to each other, such as telephones, faxes, computers, and the internet.

community—all the people living in one place.

environment—the things around us, our surroundings.

locality—the area around a settlement.

nomad—a member of a community of wandering people who live in temporary shelters.

pedestrian—a person traveling on foot.

refugee—a person forced to move because of danger, such as wars, fighting, floods, or famine.

resort—a place visited by people on vacation.

rural—a word describing things or places in the countryside.

service—providing a need for people living in a community.

settlement—a place where people have settled, such as a village, town, or city.

suburb—the outskirts of a city where people live.

unemployed—being without a job.

urban—a word used to describe things in a town or city.

utilities—basic services such as water, gas, and electricity.

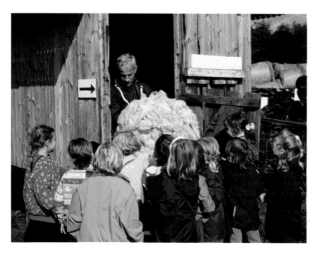

Find Out More

Take a look at these books & websites:

Books:
Geography for Fun: People and Places (Stargazer Books)

Websites:
www.un.org • www.unicef.org •
• www.europeanchildrensnetwork.org

S PECIAL • NEEDS

Services are for everyone. People who have disabilities must be able to move easily around a village, a crowded town, or a city. Look in your area. Are there wheelchair ramps at the library? Does the pedestrian crossing beep to alert people who cannot see?

INDEX

Photocredits

Abbreviations: l-left, r-right, b-bottom, t-top, c-center, m-middle

Front cover tl, 5ml, 6ml — Stockbyte. Front cover tr, 3b, 4 both, 5tr, 8tl, 8br, 9r, 10br, 11tl, 12-13, 14tr, 15bl, 15br, 16mr, 18tr, 19br, 28br — Corel. Front cover bl, back cover, 7mr, 9l, 16bm, 19tl, 19bl, 20bl, 20br, 21 both, 22mr, 24 both, 25bl, 26t, 28-29, 29br, 30bm, 31bl — Photodisc. Front cover br, 2-3, 6mr, 17t, 19mtr, 19mbr, 26br, 30br — Corbis. Front cover inset, 6tl, 19mbl — Digital Vision. 1, 7ml, 11tr, 11bl, 12tl, 12br, 13mr, 18bl, 19mtl, 19tr, 23mb, 23br, 25c, 27b, 30tr — Flat Earth. 5br, 15tr, 19ml, 20tr, 23tl —PBD. 10, 17br, 22t, 22ml, 27mr, 30-31 — Digital Stock. 11br — Comstock. 14b — John Deere. 27tl, 27tr — Federal Emergency Management Agency.